# Trauma to Triumph

# *Never Give Up*

BY LERONZO WILLIAMS

# Table of Contents

FOREWORD...........................................................- 4 -

INTRODUCTION .................................................- 7 -

DEDICATION ......................................................- 13 -

CHAPTER ONE: HUMBLE BEGINNINGS ....................- 16 -

CHAPTER TWO: DEEP IN ........................................- 29 -

CHAPTER THREE: LOCKED IN .................................- 42 -

CHAPTER FOUR: FROM STATE TO STATE ................- 57 -

CHAPTER FIVE: THE AWAKENING............................- 70 -

CHAPTER SIX: THE POWER OF ENVIRONMENT.....- 85 -

CHAPTER SEVEN: FROM TRAUMA TO TRIUMPH ....- 97 -

CHAPTER EIGHT: ONWARD AND UPWARD ............- 107 -

ABOUT THE AUTHOR .........................................- 113 -

# FOREWORD

With great honor, I introduce you to this life-changing book, *Trauma to Triumph: Never Give Up*. In these pages, you will embark on a journey with the author, Leronzo "Zo" Williams, as he shares his personal growth story. This self-help book will undoubtedly inspire you and enrich your mind. What sets this story apart is the trials the author had to overcome, the wisdom he gathered, and the practical strategies he has gained from his experiences. Far too often, we hear of people's experiences that leave us feeling sympathetic but not inspired. But Zo's narrative is different. It is a call to action, a beacon of hope that ignites a fire within the reader, urging you to confront your limitations and become the full realization of the person you were created to be.

You see, Zo's path had a lot of obstacles that would have broken most spirits – think teenage fatherhood, gang violence, and incarceration – but Zo refused to be defined by his circumstances. Although these realities trapped him in a vicious cycle of self-destruction and hate, he forged a path toward his deepest purpose, emerging stronger and wiser.

What I find most remarkable about his struggle is how he turned his past traumas into fuel for a brighter future. Like a phoenix, he arose from his ashes. He chose not to remain captive of his bad experiences; instead, he boldly took accountability for his role in co-creating the chaos that was confining him to poverty. He owned his mess and now he has a message! As you will notice, accountability and self-awareness are the keys to the door of freedom.

These pages show how he destroyed his old, self-limiting belief systems and formed a new, empowered identity. From a young hustler without direction, he became a devoted husband, father, entrepreneur, and community leader. His inspiring growth proves the human spirit can survive even the most daunting circumstances.

This book is a comprehensive guide, a treasure chest of wisdom, and a set of time-tested principles that will transform your life if you let it. Zo does not simply recount his life on these pages; he masterfully weaves in the necessary personal development strategies that serve as the foundation of his growth. From being focused and disciplined to the transformative power of mentorship and the renewal of the mind, each chapter will equip you with the tools necessary to change your life.

As you read these pages, I implore you to approach the journey with an open heart and mind. Allow the story to shine on the areas of your life ripe for growth and reinvention. Lean into the discomfort of self-reflection, for it is only by confronting the darkest corners of our being that we can truly step into the light of our greatest self. Indeed, that is the true power of this book - it speaks to the greatness that lies dormant within every one of us.

Zo's story is a clear call, urging you to shed the shackles of self-doubt, fear, and limiting beliefs that have kept you from fully embracing your destiny. It is a battle cry for you to rise, grab the wheels of your life, and hit the ground running.

So, as you start this journey, I invite you to let go of all fears and worries. Approach this book with a beginner's mind, ready to be challenged, inspired, and provoked into action. Within these pages, you will find the path to your rebirth - a blueprint for transforming trauma into triumph and never giving up on the limitless potential you possess. The time for excuses and worries has passed. The time to awaken the sleeping giant within you is now. So, turn the page, dive into Zo's story, and allow it to be the spark that ignites your journey from Trauma to Triumph. The future you've been dreaming of is closer than you think.

**Elgen Mcferren Jr**

*Professional Speaker, Author, and Coach*

# INTRODUCTION

"Our lives are not determined by what happens to us, but by how we react to what happens; not by what life brings to us, but by the attitude we bring to life." **- Wade Boggs**

In this book, "Trauma to Triumph: Never Give Up," I offer a close view into my journey from the streets to becoming a respected entrepreneur and community leader. Throughout this book, I'll share the tools of faith, focus, mentorship, and discipline that changed my destiny. Let me take you back to my roots in Mt. Vernon, Illinois - a small town where I came of age.

At the age of 17, my life took an unexpected turn. I became a father. Imagine being a kid yourself, and then suddenly you're thrown into the world of parenthood. I was burdened with responsibilities far beyond my years. I had little to no resources, limited job prospects, and no support systems. I found myself seduced by the temptation of the streets and the promise of fast money in the drug trade. Like so many young men, I got caught up in the hustle. The streets became my teacher, father, and, ultimately, my captor.

I found myself being shot not once but twice on two separate occasions. The first shooting was an incident where my child's mother took a bullet as well. As if that trauma wasn't enough, I also witnessed the painful murders of my best friend up close. Then, in 2015 on Christmas Day, I received a call that my brother had got killed. Most people would have been shattered by any one of these experiences.

But looking back, I realize that our decisions dictate our destinies far more than chances or circumstances. Those shootings were markers on my life's path.

Faith became my anchor during those difficult times. Through perseverance, I found the courage to press on when the odds seemed impossible, creating a belief in the possibility of a brighter tomorrow. I had to relentlessly re-invest in the most valuable asset - my mind.

From the teachings of spiritual masters, mentors, and self-reflection, I learned that our outer world is just a reflection of our thoughts. To experience real change, I had to reinvent myself through disciplined self-work. Little by little, I peeled back the layers of hostility, conditioning, and beliefs that had kept me in chains. Truth be told, I'm still a work in progress.

The process started with a lot of serious self-reflection: I had to dig deep. I had to confront the hard truths about how I had a part in co-creating the painful problems that I had endured. I could start the change by taking responsibility for my actions and rejecting the temptation of the victim mentality. I put myself in those situations, so I had to get myself out of them. That awakening sparked an intense hunger for personal growth. I changed my self-image, dismantled the identity I had formed from the streets, and changed my life to suit not where I was but where I wanted to be. One thing I know now is that no one can consistently behave in a manner that's inconsistent with how they see themselves.

In cases where I had once perceived myself as merely a hustler, a product of my environment, I began envisioning myself as a better man - a leader, an entrepreneur, an example of growth for my community. Les Brown said, "What you think about, you bring about." I activated new levels of creativity and resourcefulness by upgrading my mind.

With discipline as my compass, I charted a new course. I became relentless in correcting myself. I built habits that reinforced the vision of what I wanted and not what I was running from. An unshakeable determination formed within me - the desire to keep pushing forward no matter what happens. I became a hungry student, searching for

life's wisdom through mentors, books, seminars -
anything that could push my growth further and
broaden my perspectives. It was a beautiful process:
the more I opened my mind to learning, the more my
possibilities expanded. Immersing myself in the
environments of entrepreneurs and high achievers
allowed me to integrate their standards unconsciously
into my life.

Each day was a brick over another; purposeful
thoughts and actions aligned with my dreams of
prosperity and peace. I doubled down on developing
skills, pursuing education, and finding opportunities
that channeled my energy into positive creation rather
than the destructive cycles of the past.

Slowly but surely, results accumulate through the
law of cause and effect. You reap what you sow. And
truly, I was reaping fantastic rewards from all the
good habits I'd been building. The more I invested in
building my mind and habits, the more I experienced
breakthroughs across multiple areas of my life.
Financial streams opened for me, from real estate,
stock investing, and entrepreneurship. More
importantly, I healed my relationships and became
the devoted husband and father I knew I was meant
to be.

One of my mentors, Elgen Mcferren, once gave me a powerful piece of advice that has become a guiding light: "If you ever have doubts about who to help, help who you used to be." This wisdom is the sole reason I wrote this book. We all can relate to the universal human experience of struggling against our circumstances, belief systems, and patterns of self-sabotage. We all get stuck in cages - some of our own making, others constructed by our circumstances. But in every one of us lies the perfection of who we are meant to be - but this revelation requires activation.

At this stage of my life, my greatest wish is to ignite that awakening for you and every person I come across through the pages of this book and every other possible means. I'm here to shake up any false beliefs and environmental limitations you've accepted as permanent realities.

Consider this book as your guiding light, leading you out of stagnation and into the cocoon of your rebirth. I'll map out the principles and strategies that helped me out of my darkness - the actionable insights about mind, habit formation, mentorship, and more. My life will exemplify what's possible when you commit to change wholeheartedly. You'll wrestle with tough questions. You'll ask yourself, *who am I? What untruths have I unconsciously accepted about my capabilities and worth? What habits have I formed that don't align with my aspirations?*

Let's be real, getting critically honest with yourself won't be easy, but knowing who you are is essential for your growth. With my guidance and life experience, I'll show you how to destroy the boundaries holding you back. We'll tackle the false beliefs, lack of accountability, fears, and bad habits that have kept you stuck in the mud of old traumas and disappointments. Then, we will discuss how to get out of the rut.

Are you ready to change your life and finally experience the freedom and fulfillment you deserve? Then let's keep moving.

# DEDICATION

This book is dedicated to my mother, Rosie Moore, because there would be no me without her. Growing up in my early years, I was hard-headed, but she stayed with me, teaching me the difference between right and wrong. When she saw me going down the wrong path, she urged me to make a positive changes in my life, including encouraging me to attend a barber school.

Back then, I thought I knew everything. But my mother was always there for me, she stayed with me through thick and thin. She was there for me when I found myself in hospital beds and jail cells. I remember the last time I was incarcerated, she came to visit me and said she was stressing hard and losing weight. At that moment, I knew it was time to change. That was my wake-up call.

I know things were hard for her in the '80s and '90s, trying to raise a boy into a man all on her own. So, everything I do now means something to me. People said I'd be dead or locked up for life, but at this stage of my life, I'm proud to know my last name is now an asset. Regardless of what I was going through, my mother always said, "This is my boy, and I'm going to hold him down." Now, I'm here as a pre-multimillionaire and every move I make means something to me. I've seen her work the same job for over 30 years. So every day of the week, Sunday to Saturday, I grind hard to change that.

I also dedicate this book to my wife, Chevala Williams. She has stood by me since I was 20 years old, no matter my condition. She always respected herself and me, and she has been there for all my kids, even the ones who aren't biologically hers. I love her so much for that. She has always kept me grounded. When I was in barber school, I remember days when I didn't have any money, but she woke me up every day and gave me gas money to get to school, her car, and lunch money. My wife has always been a hard worker. She was working two jobs while pregnant with our twins, but I was young and lost in the street life, thinking about myself. I have since retired her from working anywhere else; she is now the director at our school, WILLIAMS BARBER ACADEMY, and the owner of WILLIAMS CONSULTING GROUP.

This book is also dedicated to my little sister, Vasheffia Williams. She has been my constant support since childhood. She has always been there for me. Whenever I needed her help, she was there. I remember her covering for me when I came home late as a teenager, and she would unlock the door for me so our parents wouldn't find out. I used to have her holding and driving things she shouldn't have been around, but now that has changed. For the last 12 years, she has been helping me unlock doors to success, holding down legal things like the empire, dealing with all our tenants, and paying all the bills. I haven't seen a bill in the last 5 years; if it has something to do with our empire, she takes care of all that. She loves me so much that she has never called me by my name; she only calls me brother.

Last but not least, I am dedicating this to my mentor, Elgen Mcferren. He has been guiding me for almost a year now, and when I say he delivers in what he does, he over-delivers tenfold. Just a year and a half ago, I was always doubting myself about pretty much everything. But since he came into my life, I am now a public speaker, author, credit repair company owner, finance educator, life/business coach, and school owner. He's steadily adding more and more things for me to have in my arsenal. He has been nothing but GREAT to my family and I since I met him. He has opened my mind in ways I never thought possible, and to top it all off, he believes in me.

# CHAPTER ONE:
# HUMBLE BEGINNINGS

"You can't go back and change the beginning, but you can start where you are and change the ending."- **C.S. Lewis**

You might have heard people say *how you start is how you'll finish*. But this couldn't be farther from the truth, otherwise I wouldn't be here today. I believe the opposite: *It doesn't matter how you start; it's how you finish.* This means the outcome is what truly counts, not the beginning. Think about it like a project or a challenge, the beginning might seem tough, but what's important is that you keep going. The difficulties we face in the process ultimately lead to goals being achieved.

Focusing on the final goal is more important than being discouraged by temporary challenges or failures. Things don't happen to you; they happen for you. I'm reminded of this quote by Samuel Lover that states: "Circumstances are rulers of the weak, but they are instruments of the wise."

The word *circumstances* comes from *circumference* - the boundary of a circle or what surrounds you while you stand inside those conditions. If you feel your circumstances are unbearable, then it's time for you to step out of the circle of confusion. Start moving, start improving, and start shifting into different environments and *circles of influence*. Improve yourself because your character growth will determine the height of your personal growth.

I vividly recall hearing that my first child was on the way at age 17. Yes, 17! I was hit with a whirlwind of emotions. Fear, and anxiety, came at once as I battled with the weight of present reality. My first thought was *my mama is going to be pissed*. But more importantly, how could I possibly care for a child when I was practically a child myself? I had no resources or income. At the time, I was hanging out, wandering without purpose. Weed and alcohol were my escape. Forget diapers, baby clothes, and formula - I could barely afford a bag of weed most days. But feeling desperate to provide, I decided to join the hustlers in my neighborhood who were into the local drug trade. It wasn't a moral decision by any means. I didn't even think to consider if it was right or wrong. But given my circumstances, it didn't feel wrong at the time. And just like that, my life as a D-Boy started. This was how I began the grind to stack up enough money to buy my first 8-ball of crack to flip on the streets.

Looking back, that path was nowhere near a straight line to a come-up. It was an uphill battle with twists and turns, low profits, and harsh lessons. I had run-ins with the law, caught up in more fights than I care to remember, and even found myself in shootouts. A constant cycle of ups and downs, wins and losses - each day of trouble led to another day of trauma. I'd already been expelled from school due to the distractions. Being a hustler came with a cost - the price of learning a game through fire. There was a day when reality truly hit me. My baby mama needed about $300 for the deposit on an apartment in the neighborhood projects.

Even though I was selling dope, I was still broke, I didn't have $100 to my name, let alone $300. My expenses always exceeded my income - a clear sign I lacked focus and financial discipline.

Back then, I lacked any kind of discipline. Then, the final blow came when I caught her kissing another man. When I confronted her, she lashed out with cruel words that rocked me: "What do you mean? You can't do anything for me. You can't help me! You're broke, man!" At that moment, I felt shattered and disrespected. But more importantly, I felt a raging fire inside being fanned and fed. A hunger to level up by any means necessary. I had to find a way to turn this game around. I sat down later that night, wrestling with the hurt and confusion in darkness and quiet.

How could I be barely making it on the streets while others were visibly winning - getting the cars, jewelry, and living that flossed-out lifestyle? I knew I had to find the answers ... there were things I didn't quite understand about this game.

That's when I reached out to an OG, who was fresh out of eight years in prison but already living large. When I asked him for the secret to his success, his response was simple: "Stack, save, and flip before you spend." This guy broke it down - he went a full 6 months without spending a dime from his hustle. No splurging, no wasting. He got a burger here and there to sustain himself, but every other dollar got reinvested into building up his cycle of buying and cooking up more products to expand his operation. He drilled into me the importance of having clear goals and powerful reasons to motivate the daily grind. "What's your target? How much are you chasing? And why are you doing this - to be a street star, or is this about providing for your family and making a real way out of this life?"

His words struck a chord within me. From that day, I applied his advice rigorously. I set an ambitious goal, got focused, and reinvested every cent towards growth. Within 4 months of discipline, restraint, and consistent action - I made my first $10,000, it was the start of building a life on the street. I didn't realize it at the time, but I had stumbled upon some of the key principles for success in any arena:

1. Clarity - Getting crystal clear on my *Why* and setting specific targets for what I wanted to achieve. That big reason became the fuel.

2. Focus - Eliminating distractions and channeling all my energy into income-generating activities. No more senseless spending or short-term pleasure seeking.

3. Sacrifice - Having the self-discipline to delay gratification and operate at a deficit, then reinvesting profits relentlessly until explosive growth occurs.

For a moment, try to think about how applicable those steps are to any goal - whether building a business, getting your desired body, or mastering a craft. This is a piece of ancient wisdom about transitioning from dreaming about success to operating in a success mindset. The problem was even though I was now operating at a high level in the streets, I was still playing a losing game.

When you set out to hustle and grind through unlawful activities, you'll inevitably hit a glass ceiling. I had started flipping that $10,000 repeatedly, but found myself getting pulled into increasingly dangerous situations. And in crime, more money means taking bigger risks and facing even greater fears. It leads to more confrontations with the other dealers, more high-stakes dealings with reckless people, and regular run-ins with law enforcement, robbers, etc. Sure, money was now stacking up, but at what cost? My activities weren't just accelerating me towards potential lockup or death. They were also separating me from my values, integrity, and self-respect. I'd gone from being desperate to provide for my family to now being an actual detriment to the family unit itself, not just mine.

I didn't understand until a few things happened - self-inflicted gut punches that were wake-up calls to my soul. First, I got shot again in yet another street clash, but this time, the bullets struck my child's mother in the crossfire, too. I've never felt lower as a man than looking into her eyes as she bled on the pavement because of my lifestyle choices. Soon after I witnessed my best friend get murdered right before my eyes. Next I lost my brother to gun violence a in separate incident. The grief was unbearable, made heavier by the reality that I was walking that same doomed path every single day. I was flirting with the same expiration date.

Those losses should've shaken me free from the self-destructive cycles for good. But growing up in that world, we get desensitized to violence and near-death experiences. The harsh conditioning of the streets numbs you from feeling any of the hurt too deeply.

The OGs kicked game about being tough, staying hard, and never showing weakness or vulnerability. *Can't stop, won't stop* becomes more than a mantra - it's a way of life, a form of psychological brainwashing that forbids you from even considering a better path because that's considered quitting. So, I powered through the trauma. I carried on with the hustle, working harder and making even more money, which only plunged me deeper into the darkness.

The more money I obtained through hustling, the more I felt trapped in that toxic lifestyle cycle. My hunger for material things and a false sense of status had me ignoring the fact that my spirit was dissolving slowly. Do you know that old analogy about the frog being slowly boiled alive? It wasn't dropped straight into boiling water, where it would instantly try to escape. Instead, it was placed in room temperature water and the temperature was gradually increased until the situation became fatal. That's precisely how the streets had grasped me in its unforgiving grip. The money, drugs, violence - it all started feeling strangely *normal* to my warped perspective. I became numb and desensitized to the trauma unfolding all around me simply because that backdrop of challenge and conflict was all I'd ever known.

The flashes of insight came only briefly, like lightning strikes illuminating the dark prison I'd constructed around my mind. Deep down, a nagging voice would try to convince me that I deserved more from this life than a temporary high followed by a sudden death or a life sentence. But whenever that voice spoke up, I swiftly drowned it out with the paralyzing thoughts of:

*This is just how it is ...*

*Everybody I know is living this life ...*

*At least I'm getting money ...*

*If I leave the streets, what else am I gonna do?*

The environmental brainwashing was potent. Trying to contemplate bettering myself was similar to a slave daring to fantasize about freedom. It wasn't allowed in the mental matrix of my world at that time. Until one day, something inside of me finally snapped. Maybe the universe gave me one last forceful shove toward my calling before I self-destructed completely. Whatever it was, it sparked the tipping point of my journey. I vividly remember having a candid conversation with God. Looking up at the heavens, I cried out something like:

"Man, if You're out there like they say ... I can't keep going on like this. I'm losing myself more each day I remain in these streets. My vices and this toxic lifestyle are a far worse prison than any cell could ever be."

"If You give me a real chance to start over, to reclaim my humanity and my purpose, I'll pour every ounce of energy into being the man You created me to be. Just grant me the strength and wisdom to find my way out before it's too late."

Looking back, I know that heartfelt prayer was the catalyst for an awakening that would utterly transform my life's path. Some call it a spiritual renewal. Others might call it a rebirth into a new state of consciousness. Either way, I began intentionally pulling back the veil of lies, generational curses, and brainwashing that had blinded me for so many years. Stepping out of the mental fog, I could finally figure out how my warped conditioning, toxic beliefs, and crippling negative self-image had fueled a brutal cycle of self-sabotage. As I peeled back these layers, I came face-to-face with two hugely unsettling truths:

1. The only person stopping me from elevating out of the streets was MYSELF. My choices, behavior, and mindset deficiencies were the anchors weighing me down in an ocean of dysfunction and negativity.

2. If I genuinely craved real and permanent change, it had to begin from the inside out before any lasting external changes could take root.

With raw clarity, I realized my quest for survival and respect had been rooted in the most detrimental form of self-hatred possible. Not only did I willfully keep engaging in activities that compromised my morals, integrity, and quality of life ... I had held a fundamentally low perception of my worth and capabilities. This wake-up call erased the self-imposed glass ceilings on my potential. No longer was I condemned to be a spectator in the movie of my own life. I could rewrite the entire script, casting myself as the heroic leading man I'd been born to become.

Chapter Summary

The chapter highlights how the author's desperate attempt to provide for his family led the author down a path of illegal activities, violence, and self-destructive choices. However, it also underscores the key principles of clarity, focus, sacrifice, and delayed gratification that initially allowed him to operate at a high level on the streets. Tragedy after tragedy, from being shot to losing loved ones, should have been wake-up calls. However, the author portrays how the harsh conditions of the street life had desensitized him, making it difficult to pursue a better path. The turning point came when he had a pivotal moment of reckoning, realizing that his mindset and behavior were the anchors weighing him down. This awakening allowed him to confront two major truths - that he was his biggest obstacle, and that real change required an inside-out approach to reprogramming his beliefs and self-image.

## Reflection Questions

1. Just like the author, how are your environment and circumstances influencing the trajectory of your life?

_____

_____

_____

_____

2. Despite operating from a scarcity mindset, the author stumbled on the principles of success (clarity, focus, sacrifice). How could applying those same principles in a positive context fuel legitimate growth in your circumstance?

_____

_____

_____

_____

_____

"The difficulties we face in the process ultimately lead to goals being achieved. Focusing on the final goal is important rather than being discouraged by temporary challenges or failures."

# CHAPTER TWO:
# DEEP IN

"The streets are full of promises, but they rarely deliver on them." - **Anonymous**

While the streets may promise fast money and respect, the true cost is often far greater than one would expect. As a young boy, the streets seemed like the quickest way to achieve my desired life. The allure of stacks of cash, flashy possessions, and reputation as a seasoned hustler fed my ego and fueled my ambition. I thought I was on the express lane to my desired life, the ultimate shortcut to the American Dream.

Little did I know I was chasing an illusion and falling into a tricky trap. The streets have a way of seducing the vulnerable, greedy, and desperate. They lure you in with the promise of easy riches, convincing you that you can outsmart the system and come out unscathed. But beneath the surface lies a reality that is evil and unforgiving. The streets are designed to keep you in a never-ending cycle of false victories and painful losses. As I began to climb the ranks, an OG took me under his wings, sharing the inside scoop on maximizing profits and outmaneuvering the competition. Despite being fresh out of prison, this OG had a wisdom that set him apart from his peers in the business. I was intrigued; I had to know how he did it. His guidance helped me get products at lower prices and save up more than I spent. With his help, I was able to undercut my rivals and become the go-to source for my customers. Suddenly, the money was flowing in like never before, I saw my first $10,000 and felt unstoppable.

### The Trap of Materialism and Ego

With my newfound stream of money, I started accumulating the trophies of street success - fancy cars, jewelry, and even properties. I wanted the world to see me as a baller, a hustler who had made it. But the more I acquired, the more I wanted. The streets had ignited a hunger within me that could never be fully satisfied. I was consumed with the desire to show off my newfound accomplishments, this made me completely disconnected from my true values and priorities. The streets had lured me into a game of ego and materialism, making me believe that my worth was measured by the things I owned, not by who I was becoming or the lives I could touch.

As time went by, I got caught up in the web of false beliefs and the illusion of success. The adrenaline rush that came with pulling off successful drug runs further tricked me into thinking I was on top and winning. I convinced myself that I was untouchable, immune to the risks that plagued others in the game. But the truth is, no one can outrun the consequences of their actions forever. The streets are filled with treachery and violence, and sooner or later, they always catch up with you.

One thing the streets do well is give you an illusion of control. The harder I hustled, the less control I had. As my hustle grew, I started to lose control of my life. Paranoia, sleepless nights, and constant fear of being caught - all took a toll on my mental and emotional well-being. I had traded my peace of mind for the promise of money and power, and the streets were slowly but surely chipping away at my soul. I thought I was the master of my destiny, but in reality, I had enslaved myself to the very system that I had tried to exploit. The streets always had a way of twisting my perception, convincing me that I was in charge when, in fact, I was just a pawn in a much larger game. Fortunately, I was granted God's grace to see and do things differently. The truth is that all illusions can vanish through awareness and accountability.

*The Cost of Survival*

The streets are not kind to those who dare to challenge them. As I navigated the streets, I was forced to confront the harsh realities of violence, betrayal, and the ever-present threat of losing everything. Witnessing the aftermath of shootouts and having loved ones caught in the crossfire - these experiences should have been wake-up calls, but the streets had a way of desensitizing me, pushing me to double down on my hustling efforts. The advice from the O.G's urging me to "triple my hustle" to honor those I had lost only strengthened the cycle of self-destruction. I had become so entrenched in the toxic mindset of the streets that I had lost sight of my values and humanity along the way.

*The Emptiness of Material Wealth*

Even as I reached new heights of a false sense of success, I felt an ever-growing void. Something was missing. The material processions I had amassed did nothing to fill the spiritual and emotional emptiness I was experiencing. I had sacrificed my dignity, integrity, and sense of purpose in pursuing this twisted version of the American Dream. The streets had promised me fulfillment, but all they offered were empty tokens of success that could never truly satisfy the deeper yearnings of my soul.

*Confronting the Truth*

At my lowest point, I finally began to face the hard truths of the path I had chosen. I had to accept the fact that no amount of money was worth the spiritual and emotional devastation I had endured. The

American Dream I had been chasing was nothing more than a mirage, a carefully constructed illusion designed to keep me and others like me in a state of oppression. I wanted freedom, true freedom. But I had to realize that wanting it was the first step. I had to see that I was stuck in mental chains, even if I wasn't behind physical bars. Those chains were wrecking my chances of a better life because of my habits. The only difference between the people who win and those who fail lies in their habits. But like Warren Buffet said, "The chains of habits are too light to be felt until they are too heavy to be broken." The streets were never intended for me to win. They had merely wanted to exploit my ambition and desperation for their selfish desire. My true victory was in learning how to win by conquering my flaws, vices, insecurities, and selfishness.

### The Moment of Truth

In that moment of reckoning, I saw the truth; the hills I had sacrificed so much to climb were nothing more than short-lived pride. I had given away everything of true value - my self-respect, my alignment with my highest purpose, and my belief in my dignity. It was a painful realization, but it was also the first step towards reclaiming my life. I finally realized the streets were never going to lead me to true fulfillment, no matter how much wealth or status they promised. The only way forward was to shed the toxic mindset that had taken hold of me and rediscover my authentic path.

## Lessons Learned

My journey through the streets was a harsh but invaluable lesson about the dangers of chasing false promises and misguided ambitions. Here are some of the key principles I've learned:

1.   Beware of the Trap of the Streets: The streets are designed to lure in the vulnerable and desperate, offering the illusion of easy wealth and power. But the reality is that they are carefully laid traps meant to keep you in a continuous cycle of false victories and devastating losses. Anything can be your *street* - whether it's the literal streets or figurative streets of addiction, unhealthy relationships, or dead-end jobs. The key is to recognize that these streets are a trap and to find the courage and determination to get out of them. The path out may not be easy, but it is worth it to escape the cycle of despair and claim your true potential.

2.   Resist the Siren Call of Materialism and Ego: The streets thrive on the allure of material possessions

and the validation of status. But true fulfillment can never be found in the endless pursuit of wealth and the approval of others. It's a trap that only leads to emptiness and disconnection from your core values. The streets promise an easy path to power and prestige, but this is all an illusion. In reality, the streets are designed to keep you constantly chasing after the next material acquisition or social validation, leaving you feeling hollow and dissatisfied. True meaning and purpose can only be found by breaking free from this toxic cycle and reconnecting with what truly matters to you. The path out may be challenging, but it is the only way to achieve genuine fulfillment and live a life aligned with your deepest values.

3. Recognize the Limits of Control: The streets may make you feel invincible, but the truth is that no one can outrun the consequences of their actions. The violence, the betrayal, and the ever-present threat of loss are the harsh realities that eventually catch up with those who think they can master the game.

4. Beware Toxic Counsel: The advice and perspectives of those entrenched in the streets can be incredibly warped, perpetuating cycles of self-destruction and disconnection from one's true values. It's crucial to cultivate a discerning mindset and surround yourself with positive, uplifting influences.

5. Seek Authentic Fulfillment: No amount of material wealth or status can ever fill the void within. True fulfillment comes from aligning your actions with your deepest values, reconnecting with your sense of purpose, and rediscovering your innate dignity and worth.

The journey through the streets has been a harsh but necessary lesson in the pursuit of true fulfillment and meaning. As you reflect on your experiences and temptations, I encourage you to heed the warnings and lessons I've shared. The streets, like many of life's temptations, may offer the promise of easy riches, short-term satisfaction, and quick fixes, but the true cost is far too high. Instead, I invite you to embark on a different path that honors your values, nurtures your spirit, and empowers you to create lasting, meaningful change.

It may not be the quickest or the most glamorous route, but it is the surest way to find the peace, purpose, and self-actualization that the streets can never provide. The choice is yours. Will you succumb to the lure of the streets, or will you have the courage to forge your authentic path? The road ahead may be challenging, but the rewards of living with integrity and purpose are unparalleled.

## Chapter Summary

This chapter serves as a cautionary tale about the dangers of succumbing to the allure of the streets - a metaphor for any temptation or pathway that promises easy riches and power but at a devastating personal cost. The author recounts his experience of being drawn into the criminal underworld, enticed by the prospect of fast money, material possessions, and status. However, he soon realized that the streets were a carefully constructed trap designed to keep him perpetually enslaved to a cycle of ego, materialism, and false control.

Despite his initial false feelings of being untouchable and a master of the system, the author ultimately faced the harsh realities of violence, betrayal, and the ever-present threat of losing everything. Even as his financial success grew, he found an emptiness within that no amount of wealth could fill. It was only through a moment of reckoning and confronting the truth that he could break free from the toxic mindset of the streets and begin the journey of reclaiming their authentic purpose and values. The key lessons emphasized include resisting the lure of materialism and ego, recognizing control limits, and seeking genuine, sustainable fulfillment over temporary validation and status.

## Reflection Questions

1.  What aspects of the streets and the temptations they offer do you relate to most in your own life experience? How have you seen these temptations manifest, even if not in the literal street life described?

_____
_____
_____
_____
_____

2.  Discuss the author's perspective on the traps of materialism and ego. How have you seen this dynamic play out in your own life or the lives of people around you? What are the dangers of becoming overly attached to material wealth and status?

_____
_____
_____
_____
_____

3.  The author discusses the facade of invincibility that can develop when navigating the streets. Reflect

on times when you may have felt a similar false sense
of control or immunity from consequences. What led
to that feeling, and how did reality end up unfolding?

_____

_____

_____

_____

_____

_____

4. How do you think the author's *Lessons Learned*
from their experience on the streets could apply to
temptations and challenges you face in your own life,
even if the specific context is different? Which of
these lessons resonates most strongly with you?

_____

_____

_____

_____

_____

5. The author emphasizes the importance of
*authentic fulfillment* over the empty promises of the
streets. What does authentic fulfillment mean to you?
How can you work towards that in your life rather

than chasing temporary or superficial sources of satisfaction?

_____

_____

_____

_____

_____

6.  Reflecting on your life experiences, what cautionary tales or wisdom would you share with others to help them avoid the pitfalls described in this chapter? What has been instrumental in helping you stay true to your values in the face of temptation?

_____

_____

_____

_____

_____

_____

"The only difference between the people who win and those who fail lies in their habits."

# CHAPTER THREE: LOCKED IN

"Your life is controlled by what you focus on."

**- Tony Robbins**

The path to true fulfillment is paved with focus, discipline, and an unwavering commitment to our goals. We are all just one bad decision away from being *locked in* - whether it's a legal consequence, a personal setback, or simply finding ourselves stuck in a cycle of bad habits.

I'll never forget the day I found myself behind bars at the age of 17, facing severe consequences for a school fight that left another guy hospitalized. It was a harsh wake-up call, a reminder that the choices we make have consequences. But as I sat in that county jail, I saw clearly that my physical imprisonment was merely a reflection of a deeper issue - a lack of mental discipline and focus. You see, the thing about life is that we're all one decision away from being arrested, whether allowing our temper to explode, engaging in reckless behavior, or simply neglecting our responsibilities. It happens to the best of us. But what truly separates those who succeed from those who stumble is their ability to respond effectively to these challenges.

## The Power of Cause and Effect

One of the biggest lessons I learned early on was the principle of cause and effect - you reap what you sow. This principle helped me understand where my problems came from and how I could fix them. However, knowing this and doing something about it are two very different things. It's easier said than done, but when it's done, life becomes easier. My physical incarceration was a direct result of my lack of mental and emotional maturity. I allowed my temper to control me, and the consequences were swift and severe. But the truth is, we are all responsible for virtually everything that happens to us. It's not about what happens to us but about how we choose to respond. You reap what you sow, right? So, if we don't like what we're reaping, we must improve what we're sowing. You can't plant a poison ivy tree and reap watermelon. If I want to receive kindness, I must be kind. If I want friends, I must be a friend. If I truly want to be successful, I must adopt successful habits. It's all about the choices we make.

## Unlocking the Doors of Our Prison

To break free from the things that arrest our progress and stop us from growing, we must learn to lock in with intense focus and stay disciplined. We must be willing to let go of thoughts that hold us back and distractions that trap us in a cycle of self-sabotage and unfulfilled potential. It all starts with our thinking - how do we perceive ourselves? Do we see ourselves as winners or losers? We must understand that our thoughts shape the foundation of our lives. You might dream of being a millionaire, but if you feel unworthy or incapable of achieving your goals, those beliefs will sabotage your efforts.

*Creating a Powerful Belief System*

Once we believe in ourselves and feel confident about our abilities, we can start to build a vision for our lives. From that vision, we can set a clear, specific goal and then create a plan to achieve it. But the real magic happens when we lock in, focus, and take action. Focus and discipline are not just abstract concepts but the keys to unlocking our true potential. Look at any highly successful person, whether an athlete, a celebrity, or a business leader - they all have an unmatched level of self-discipline that has propelled them to the top of their respective fields.

On the other hand, those who are considered "failures" in life often struggle with a lack of self-discipline. I know this firsthand, as my lack of discipline with managing my temper is what landed me in jail in the first place. It's an eye-opening realization but also a powerful opportunity for growth.

*The Process of Success (and Failure)*

Success and failure are not just isolated events - they are the products of a process, a series of choices and actions that reflect the outcomes we experience. When I got an F in a class or on a test, it wasn't just some random occurrence - it was the result of not studying, not paying attention in class or prioritizing distractions over preparation. The same is true for success. The highly successful person didn't just *become* successful overnight - it resulted from a disciplined process of getting up early, managing their time, seeking out mentors, and consistently taking actions aligned with their goals.

The process might seem tough but it's actually promising and profitable. For instance, if I asked you to eat a raw egg you'd be like, hell no, I'm good. If I instructed you to eat a cup of sugar, salt, and flour, you'd immediately object, thinking, is he trying to kill me? See, all of these items individually sound gross to consume. However, collectively, those are the ingredients for a delicious pound cake. So, when life serves you a little defeat, setback, or betrayal, remember: these are all magnificent ingredients that can produce a successful man or woman. Trust the process.

*The Power of Focus*

"When every physical and mental resource is focused, one's power to solve a problem multiplies tremendously."

**- Norman Vincent Peale**

One of the keys to unlocking your desired success is intense focus. The most successful person is an average man or woman who stays focused, disciplined, and executed on their goal. To be disciplined, you have to stay focused and to focus, you must be disciplined. To execute any high quality plan or goal, you must have both.

Everything you accomplish in your personal or professional life comes down to how well you can concentrate. How focused are you? The lack of focus is the main reason that prevents people from achieving their goals or becoming their best selves. When you concentrate on your goal, your actions and thoughts become specifically targeted toward accomplishing that objective, giving you the traction and momentum you need to succeed.

Also, allowing ourselves to become distracted delays our progress and threatens to derail our destiny entirely. Think of focus like a muscle - it can be developed and strengthened through practice and determination. And the key to building that focus muscle is clarity. Clarity is all about making things concise and easy to understand.

Having mental clarity means thinking, staying focused, and making good decisions without feeling confused or distracted. It's about being able to think quickly and understand things well. In our darkest moments, we must have clarity of vision to see the light in a dark situation.

*Cultivating Clarity*

The greater your clarity regarding your version of success and what you would like to do in life, the more likely you are to stay on track and manage the events that bring you closer to your goal. For example, if you have a clear goal to save $1,000 a month, eating out daily, drinking weekly, and splurging will take you in the opposite direction. However, meal prepping, cutting out unnecessary coffee runs, and developing a budget will move you closer to your goal. Spending more than you earn is not sustainable; this habit causes you financial trouble. To truly build your finances, you need to lower your expenses, increase your income, and make investments. It's that simple.

Having a clear plan on the steps you need to take makes it easier to avoid procrastination and stay focused. Clarity is perhaps the most important concept in purpose and productivity, as it allows us to filter out the noise and maintain commitment to the things that truly matter.

Just imagine a world-class athlete laser focused on achieving their goal of winning a championship. Their every thought and action is geared towards that purpose. They don't allow themselves to be sidetracked by small concerns or outside distractions - they are locked in, fully present, and relentless in their pursuit of excellence. I was broke because I was unclear about how money worked. I was frustrated about being a legitimate entrepreneur because I had no clarity about the process and its benefits.

However, exposure creates expansion, so once I became clear on what I needed to do, what mentors I needed to attain, the books I needed to read, and more, I had clarity on what action to take to achieve the personal and professional results I desired.

*The Power of Visualization*

In addition to cultivating laser-sharp focus and intense discipline, unlocking our true potential is greatly achieved through visualization. When you vividly imagine yourself achieving your goals, your brain starts to believe you can do it. For example, I visualized myself as a successful hustler when I was in the streets. I saw the gilts, the glimmer, the money, and the honey in detail. This helped me align my actions with my thoughts.

As Les Brown said, "What you think about, you bring about." By visualizing my success, I was able to make it happen. Also, when I envisioned myself as a successful businessman, a great father, husband, and community leader, my entire self-image changed, changing my behavior and life. See, no one can ever rise above their self-image. The way you see yourself determines how you move. Your self-image is the blueprint from which your life will be built. It dictates your beliefs, actions, and, ultimately, your outcomes. No matter how hard you strive, you'll never rise above the limits you've set for yourself in your mind. The interesting part is that I was down because of my poor self-image, and I grew because of a renewed self-image.

Successful people across all walks of life, from athletes to entrepreneurs, have long utilized the power of visualization to bridge the gap between their current reality and their desired future. They take the time to clearly define their objectives and then build a detailed mental picture of themselves accomplishing great things. This practice not only boosts their belief in the possibility of achieving their goals but also guides their actions with a heightened sense of purpose and determination.

When we see ourselves succeeding, doing the work required to make that vision a reality becomes easier.

*The Power of Habit*

"The chains of habits are too light to be felt until they are too heavy to be broken."

**- Warren Buffet**

The power of habit will make or break you. The difference between the people who win and the people who lose in life often comes down to the difference in their habits. Successful people have cultivated successful habits, while the unsuccessful have developed habits that hold them back. Because at the end of the day, what you do habitually will determine who you become permanently.

To succeed, you must start building habits that support your goals - waking up early, reading, exercising, and managing your time effectively. These may seem like small, insignificant actions, but they are the building blocks of a life well-lived. When I had habits of smoking or drinking daily, habits of spending money I didn't have, and habits of not reading or working out, my life was disorganized and unproductive.

However, when I started working out frequently, I had more money. I had more because getting fit required self-discipline, which showed up in other areas of my life. I grew more patient, and I developed better relationships with new people. I once heard someone say that we don't decide our future; we decide our habits, and our habits decide our future. Facts! See, you get better results when you develop better habits because you can't receive new blessings with old structures. I realized that my success and progress were limited based on my habits. If I wanted more, I had to become more.

Chapter Summary

This chapter explains the importance of focus, discipline, and commitment in achieving goals and unlocking true potential. Drawing from a personal experience of facing severe consequences due to a lack of discipline, the author emphasizes the principle of cause and effect - that our outcomes are directly tied to our choices and behaviors. To break free from our self-created prisons, the author stresses the need to cultivate a strong, empowering mindset and clear vision for the future. Focus is the key, likened to a muscle that is developed through consistent practice.

Habits are highlighted as the foundation of focus and discipline, with the author asserting that our habitual patterns ultimately determine our long-term success or failure. The chapter encourages readers to examine their habits and behaviors and take proactive steps to replace unproductive patterns with those that support their goals. Through a series of reflection questions, the reader is invited to identify areas of their life that feel locked in and explore strategies for developing the focus, discipline, and commitment required to forge a path of lasting fulfillment and achievement.

## Reflection Questions:

1.  What are the specific areas of your life where you feel *locked in?* What are the root causes of these issues, and how can you begin to address them?

_____

_____

_____

_____

_____

_____

2.  Examine your current belief system - do you see yourself as a winner, or a loser? How can you shift your mindset to one of empowerment and possibility?

_____

_____

_____

_____

_____

3.  Identify one or two key goals you want to achieve in the near future. What steps can you take to build laser-sharp focus and unwavering discipline to make those goals a reality?

_____

_____

_____

_____

_____

_____

4.   What are some of the habitual patterns or behaviors in your life that are holding you back from reaching your full potential? How can you start replacing those unproductive habits with ones that support your growth and success?

_____

_____

_____

_____

_____

5.   Reflect on a time when you experienced a significant setback or consequence. How can you apply the lessons of cause and effect to prevent similar challenges from arising in the future?

_____

_____

_____

_____

6.   The path to true fulfillment is paved with focus, discipline, and a steadfast commitment to our

goals. If we develop the right mindset and build powerful habits, we can break free from the prisons we've created for ourselves and unlock our true potential. It's time to take control of our lives and forge the future we know we can achieve.

_____

_____

_____

_____

_____

_____

_____

"Success and failure are not just isolated events - they are the products of a process, a series of choices and actions that reflect the outcomes we experience."

# CHAPTER FOUR: FROM STATE TO STATE

"We are all anxious to improve our conditions, but we are unwilling to improve ourselves. Therefore, we remain bound." - **James Allen**

As discussed earlier, achieving genuine fulfillment and success requires a foundation built upon focus, discipline, and a willingness to confront the consequences of our choices and actions. But the journey doesn't end there. To thrive in an ever-changing world, we must also cultivate the skill of adaptability - the ability to navigate challenges, seize new opportunities, and reshape our circumstances.

*The Illusion of Success*

Superficially, the hustle appeared to be a winning formula. I had all the trappings of success - the fancy clothes, the flashy jewelry, the expensive cars, and the entourage of women. To the casual observer, I was living the dream, a true baller who had beat the odds and made it to the top. But the truth was, I was dying on the inside. The more I pushed to expand my empire, the more I jeopardized my freedom and the well-being of my own family. I was caught in a vicious cycle of self-destruction, convincing myself that my illegal activities were somehow providing for those I cared about when in reality, I was feeding a dangerous cycle of trauma and generational curses.

## The Inevitability of Consequences

Each time I engaged in street activities, I increased my chances of incarceration or becoming a victim of violence. The longer I remained entrenched in that lifestyle, the more inevitable those penalties became. It was only a matter of time before the walls would come crashing down and I would face the harsh realities of my choices. My journey from state to state on the streets symbolized the importance of adaptability and resilience in all areas of life. Just as I had to be willing to shift my geographic location and build new relationships to succeed in the drug trade, we must also be willing to adapt and evolve in our personal and professional pursuits.

## Shifting Gears: Going Legit

Fortunately, I was given a second chance at life, an opportunity to right the wrongs of my past and reshape my future. And when I finally stepped away from the streets and immersed myself in legitimate endeavors, I found that the same principles of adaptability and resilience remained essential. As I pursued a career in the barbering industry, I once again had to be willing to travel from state to state, attending seminars and workshops and seeking exclusive products and tools of the trade. This journey constantly exposed me to new knowledge, and techniques, and broadened my understanding of business practices.

*The Power of a Shifting Mindset*

The real transformation wasn't just external- it was also an internal shift, a complete overhaul of my mindset and perspective. When I was trapped in the streets, my entire worldview was tainted by the toxic hustle mentality. I saw the world as a zero-sum game, where my gain had to come at the expense of someone else's loss. However, as I began to immerse myself in legitimate businesses and surround myself with more positive influences, I started to realize that the key to success was not about dominating or exploiting others, but about constantly evolving and adapting to the changing tides of the market. It was a mindset shift that allowed me to be free from the shackles of my past and embrace a new, empowered way of thinking.

*Creating the Resilient Mindset*

This shift in mindset is perhaps one of the most crucial aspects of mastering the power of adaptability and resilience. Our state of mind is one of our most valuable assets, and it is our responsibility to protect and optimize it. It's the lens through which we view the world, the filter that determines how we interpret and respond to both challenges and opportunities that come our way. And when it comes to navigating the ebb and flow of life, a resilient mindset truly unlocks our full potential. It's the ability to bounce back from setbacks, to learn from our failures, and to continuously evolve and improve ourselves, no matter the obstacles we encounter.

*The Mindset of the Lion*

A compelling illustration of this resilient mindset can be found in the animal kingdom, with the majestic lion. Often hailed as the "King of the Jungle," the lion's dominance and success have little to do with its size or physical strength. The elephants could easily overpower the lion if they simply embraced their power and capabilities. Yet, what sets the lion apart is its unwavering sense of self-belief and its refusal to be intimidated by the perceived power of others. The lion doesn't hesitate to confront the elephant because it has an unshakable confidence in its abilities. It's a mindset of pure focus and determination - a willingness to take bold action and seize opportunities, regardless of the potential risks.

This is the kind of mindset we must develop if we truly want to thrive in a constantly changing world. It's the mindset that says, *I will not be deterred by obstacles, I will not be limited by my circumstances, and I will not be intimidated by the perceived strengths of others. I am the master of my destiny, and I will achieve my goals.*

### The Power of Action

Mindset is undoubtedly important, but it is only one piece of the puzzle. True adaptability and resilience also require a willingness to take bold, decisive action - to embrace the discomfort of the unknown and the possibility of failure in pursuit of our dreams. As the age-old saying goes, "The only way to learn how to do is through doing." We can't simply sit back and theorize about the perfect solution or the perfect timing - we have to be willing to get our hands dirty, experiment, and learn from our mistakes.

The parable of the ceramics class is a powerful example of this principle. There was a ceramics teacher who conducted an experiment where he split his classroom into groups. Group A was to specifically focus on quantity. They were simply tasked with producing as many as they could within the allotted time. Group B however was asked to specifically focus on creating the perfect pot. Who do you think had the perfect piece of pottery? While Group B - the perfect quality group - was busy obsessing over the pursuit of perfection, they didn't get much accomplished. However, Group A - the quantity group - was churning out piles of work, learning from their mistakes, correcting their behavior, and eventually producing the highest quality pieces. It's a testament to the power of action over thinking and of momentum over hesitation.

### Bouncing Back from Failure

And when we inevitably face setbacks and failures along the way, true resilience is demonstrated by those who bounce back, learn from their mistakes, and use that experience to propel themselves forward. As Bruce Lee famously said, "In great attempts, it is glorious even to fail." Failure is not something to be feared but rather an opportunity for growth and learning. The more we're willing to put ourselves out there, take calculated risks, and embrace the lessons that come from our missteps, the stronger and more adaptable we become. After all, the path to success is rarely a straight line. It's a winding journey filled with twists and turns, challenges and opportunities. And the individuals who are able to navigate that journey with grace, agility, and a resilient mindset are the ones who ultimately emerge victorious.

## A Comprehensive Approach to Adaptability and Resilience

So, what are the key principles and practices we can embrace to promote this powerful combination of adaptability and resilience? Let's dive in.

### *Embrace the Ebb and Flow*

Just as I had to deal with the constant changes in the drug trade market, we must be willing to embrace the ebb and flow of life itself. Be it changes in the economy, shifts in our industry, or personal circumstances, the ability to adapt and respond effectively is crucial. This means constantly monitoring the landscape, staying attuned to emerging trends and opportunities, and being willing to adjust our strategies and tactics as needed. It's about maintaining an attitude of flexibility and responsiveness rather than clinging to a rigid mindset.

### *Expand Your Reach*

In the same way I needed to go out of my hometown to find new suppliers and markets, we must be willing to step out of our comfort zones and explore new territories, both literally and figuratively. This could mean pursuing new educational or professional opportunities, building relationships with individuals from diverse backgrounds, or exposing ourselves to new ideas and experiences. The more we're willing to expand our horizons, the more adaptable and resilient we become.

*Embrace the Power of Action*

Finally, we must be willing to put our resilient mindset into practice to embrace the discomfort of the unknown and the possibility of failure in pursuit of our goals. As the story of the ceramics class illustrated, it's the individuals willing to take action, experiment, and learn from their mistakes who ultimately achieve the highest levels of success. This means moving forward with decisiveness and momentum rather than overthinking and hesitation. It's about trusting the process, staying focused on our objectives, and making continuous, incremental progress, even in the face of setbacks.

## Chapter Summary

This chapter emphasizes the importance of adaptability and resilience in navigating an ever-changing world and achieving lasting success. Drawing from personal experiences in the illegal drug trade, the author highlights how adaptability was crucial for successfully managing market fluctuations and expanding their reach across state lines. However, he also cautions against the false trappings of success, recognizing that their criminal empire ultimately jeopardizes their freedom and well-being. It was only when he shifted gears and pursued legitimate business endeavors and clean spiritual living that the true value of adaptability became clear.

**Reflection Questions:**

1.   Reflect on a time when you had to adapt to a significant change or challenge. What were the key strategies and mindsets that helped you navigate that transition successfully?

_____

_____

_____

_____

2.   Where in your life are you currently facing the need to expand your reach or explore new territories, whether literally or figuratively? What fears or hesitations might be holding you back, and how can you overcome them?

_____

_____

_____

_____

_____

3.   Examine your current belief system and mindset. Are there any limiting perspectives or self-doubts that are inhibiting your ability to be adaptable and resilient? How can you begin to shift your

mindset to embrace a more empowered, forward-looking perspective?

_____

_____

_____

_____

_____

_____

4.   Think of a major goal or dream you're pursuing. What specific action steps can you take today to start building momentum and pushing through the discomfort of the unknown? How can you cultivate a bias towards decisive action over stuck and stagnated thinking?

_____

_____

_____

_____

_____

_____

_____

5.   When you inevitably face setbacks or failures along the way, how can you adopt a mindset of resilience and use those experiences as opportunities

for growth and learning? What strategies can you employ to bounce back stronger than ever?

_____

_____

_____

_____

_____

_____

_____

"Our state of mind is one of our most valuable assets, and it is our responsibility to protect and optimize it. It's the lens through which we view the world, the filter that determines how we interpret and respond to both challenges and opportunities that come our way."

# CHAPTER FIVE:
# THE AWAKENING

"It's amazing how one can be sleepwalking, unaware of how deeply entrenched they are in a situation or what caused the chaos." **- Anonymous**

Throughout our journey, we've explored the significance of focus, discipline, and adaptability in achieving lasting success and fulfillment. But there is one crucial element that ties all these principles together - the power of accountability. It's natural to point fingers and blame external factors for our struggles and shortcomings. Our jobs, family backgrounds, and even past mistakes can all seem like convenient scapegoats for the confusion and unhappiness in our lives. But the hard truth is that *our actions and beliefs shape the outcomes we experience.*

## *The Myth of the Self-Made*

Legendary motivational speaker Earl Nightingale once said, "We are all self-made, but only the successful will admit it." This powerful statement cuts to the heart of the matter - we are all responsible for the direction of our lives, whether we choose to acknowledge it or not. Think about it - the self-made millionaire proudly proclaims the story of their climb out of poverty, but what about the self-made drunk, the self-made drug addict, or the person drowning in debt? They are all self-made in that their current circumstances are the direct result of their choices and behaviors.

When I embraced this truth, I let go of the victim mentality that blamed external factors like the government or racism. Hosea 4:6 of the Bible states, "My people are destroyed from the lack of knowledge." So, if I could ruin my life from the lack of knowledge, then I could build up myself and others with better information, more discipline, and a shift in my mindset.

### The Awakening

This was my reality, I had to acknowledge the fact that I was not just a *thug* or a *pusher* - I was a king, a father, a community leader, and a business owner. I had always seen myself as a successful man, feeling the essence of my greatness deep within my soul. But it was as though I had been an eagle raised in a chicken coop, unaware of my true power and purpose due to my surroundings.

Despite my natural leadership qualities, I found myself following instead of leading. I was rolling with the trends and norms of my environment instead of customizing my life based on my calling. I was experiencing trauma, confusion, and indecision because I was operating outside of my natural, authentic self. We have two types of positions: our natural and adaptive selves. Our natural self is how we function based on our purpose or life's design. You don't have to think about your thoughts or movements when functioning naturally. You are just what you are and how you are. This is called being your authentic self; this is true power. But when you function from an adaptive stance, your actions and behaviors change based on your environment or when you're being watched, observed, or under pressure. It's important to note that the reverse is also true, just like how potent you are when you operate naturally as your authentic self. The more you operate in your adaptive state, the more prone you are to depression, anxiety, and a major loss of personal power.

However, I had allowed myself to become so deeply entrenched in a toxic mindset and environment that I had lost sight of my true identity and potential. It wasn't until I took the time to examine myself and confront the beliefs and conditioning that had shaped my actions that I was able to undergo a profound awakening. I realized that I had been conditioned to believe that my people were "less than" and that to succeed, I had to embody the stereotypical images of the rapper, the dope boy, or the player.

## The Cornerstone of Success

The moment I shifted my self-image and truly saw myself for who I could be, everything started to change. I started gaining momentum in ways that yielded the results I truly wanted rather than the ones that were rejected by society. The key to this change was accountability. I had to take all things into account, and then I would be able to beat the rat race mentality and truly win for myself. I had to take full responsibility for my current circumstances, strengths and weaknesses, and the path I wanted to forge for my future.

In business, they call it the S.W.O.T analysis. This is an exercise where you closely examine your Strengths, Weaknesses, Opportunities, and Threats before investing and embarking on a venture. I couldn't hide behind excuses or external factors anymore - it was time to own my decisions and their positive and negative consequences. This process of self-examination was not easy, as it required me to confront the painful truths about my choices and behavior. But it was a necessary journey, for it was only by taking responsibility for my circumstances that I could reclaim my power and reshape my destiny.

## The Power of Ownership

True accountability means taking ownership. As the saying goes, "We come into this world looking like our parents, but we leave this world looking like our decisions." Every circumstance surrounding my life, from being incarcerated to becoming a successful business owner of multiple establishments, author, and motivational speaker, was a direct result of my choices. When we own up to our actions, decisions, and behaviors, we empower ourselves to make a real difference in our lives and the lives of others. We become more committed to our goals, bounce back from failure with renewed vigor, and are more likely to follow through on our commitments.

## The Importance of Introspection

A key part of this awakening process is the power of introspection - the ability to examine our conscious thoughts, emotions, and value systems. Introspection is a powerful tool for building emotional self-awareness and leading ourselves and others through times of change. When we evaluate ourselves, we grow in every part of our lives. Our values decide how successful we become. Our emotions are like the energy that moves us, and oftentimes, it's not what we can't do that stops us, but how we feel about a situation. When we say things like, "I don't feel like reading," "I don't feel like saving," or "I don't feel like working out," we're not acknowledging what we must and should do - we're letting our emotions dictate our actions.

However, through the practice of introspection, we can gain a deeper understanding of ourselves, our motivations, and the root causes of our behavior. This self-reflection allows us to process what we've learned and uncover the insights we need to take meaningful action and achieve the results we desire. Every day, I make sure to intentionally set aside time to reflect on my day. I ask myself questions such as *did I go as hard as I could? Did I invest time in my family as much as possible? Am I making excuses to justify my failure, or am I learning from my losses?* These questions help me stay focused on my goals and the journey ahead.

## The Foundation of Discipline

I quickly learned that achieving my goals and dreams required focus, effort, and self-control. Discipline acts as a means to setting and accomplishing a goal, bringing light to the importance of dedication and perseverance. Self-discipline is the key to unlocking our full potential. It's the ability to delay gratification in the short term to enjoy greater rewards in the long term. And it all starts with the mastery of our thoughts. When I began to manage my thoughts, I became a better manager of my life.

Because anything you mismanage, you lose. The more disciplined I became, the more I grew and the more I could accomplish. I had to be realistic with myself. Everything that I didn't have, that I didn't accomplish, and that I ever lost was in some way or another connected to my lack of discipline.

As the legendary Napoleon Hill said, "If you don't control what you think, you can't control what you do." Setting clear objectives and sticking to a plan helps us stay on track, overcome obstacles, and make steady progress toward our dreams. I've learned firsthand the power of discipline. In the past, my lack of discipline in saving money caused me financial problems. My unwillingness to read limited the ideas I could generate to create income. Also, my unwillingness to work out created health issues, weight gain, and a lack of energy. But when I became more disciplined, I saw how much it paid off. There are multiple benefits to every disciplined effort. As I began applying the principles of discipline to my life, I witnessed a major change in my financial and personal business.

A focused, intentional, proactive, and self-aware leader slowly replaced the once disorganized and reactive individual. In life, before you lead others, you must be the leader in your own life. I could feel the weight of the past begin to lift, and in its place, a newfound sense of purpose and direction began to take root.

*The Power of Mentorship*

Reflecting on the pivotal moments that sparked my change, I am struck by my mentors' profound and lasting impact on my journey. These individuals saw the spark of greatness within me, even when I was blinded by self-doubt and limiting beliefs. They stretched out their hands, pulling me from the depths of despair and guiding me toward a future of limitless possibility. One mentor, Elgen Mcferren, stands out as a true pillar of support and inspiration. Elgen had walked a remarkably similar path to mine, overcoming the challenges of a rough upbringing and the seductive pull of the streets to become a thriving entrepreneur and community leader. When we first connected, I was amazed by his belief in my potential, even as I struggled to see it within myself.

Elgen began by pushing me to dream bigger and to set goals that surpassed the boundaries of my self-imposed limitations. He often reminded me, "Zo, you have to see yourself as the successful, empowered man you are becoming. Stop entertaining other's perception of you as a product of your environment." Through his constant encouragement and strategic guidance, I slowly began to break free from the mental shackles and embrace a new, more empowered identity that was in alignment with my self-image. But Elgen's mentorship went far beyond mere cheerleading. He also held me accountable, challenging me to confront the self-sabotaging behaviors that kept me stuck in cycles of dysfunction and despair. Whether it was my tendency to overspend or my habit of making excuses, Elgen would meet my resistance with tough love, refusing to let me off the hook.

"You've got to start taking radical responsibility for your life, Zo," he would say. "No more blaming the streets or your circumstances. Those are just the cards you were dealt - now it's up to you to play them masterfully." His words cut deep, but I knew he was right. If I truly wanted to transform my life, I had to be willing to do the inner work of self-examination and personal accountability. And as I leaned into that process, the breakthroughs began to accumulate. I opened my first barber school, wrote my first book, began public speaking on major platforms, and even began exploring new avenues of personal growth, like meditation and spiritual study. With each milestone, my confidence grew, and the vision I held for my future became increasingly clear and tangible.

But Elgen's impact extended far beyond my change. He also introduced me to a powerful network of like-minded entrepreneurs, visionaries, and change-makers. It was a community that would become a vital source of support and collaboration. In these enriching spaces, I began to truly understand the power of collective growth and the importance of surrounding myself with people who shared my values and aspirations. As they say, you are the total of the five people you spend the most time with. If you consciously put yourself near people who have achieved or are achieving what you want, you put yourself on the path to accomplish your goal too.

### The Ownership Mindset

Ultimately, the awakening I experienced was all about taking full responsibility for my life. No more excuses, justifications, no one else to blame. No one was coming to save me. I alone was responsible for the quality of my life, and what I sowed, I would surely reap. It was a powerful realization that has served as the foundation for everything I've accomplished ever since. When you take complete accountability for your actions and decisions, you unlock levels of development that make you unstoppable. The path to lasting fulfillment and growth requires accountability, introspection, and discipline. By confronting our limiting beliefs and cultivating the commitment necessary to achieve our goals, we can unlock our true potential and create the future we deserve. It won't be easy, and there will be setbacks along the way. So, let's dive in, roll up our sleeves, and get to work - the future is ours to shape.

## Chapter Summary

This chapter emphasizes the role of accountability in the author's journey toward lasting success and fulfillment. He acknowledges the temptation to blame outer conditions and factors for his struggles but recognizes that his actions and beliefs have shaped the outcomes he has experienced. The author undergoes a profound *awakening*, where he confronts the painful truths about his past choices and conditioning and takes responsibility for reshaping his destiny. He learns that true accountability is about ownership - owning his decisions, his strengths, and his weaknesses. Through the power of introspection and self-examination, the author is able to shed the beliefs and behaviors that had previously held him back and embrace a newfound sense of purpose and direction. He credits the transformative influence of his mentors, who challenged him to dream bigger and take full responsibility for his life, as a major instrument in this awakening process.

## Reflection Questions

1.  In what areas of your life have you been quick to blame external factors for your struggles or shortcomings? How can you start taking more ownership and accountability for the outcomes you're experiencing?

_____

_____

_____

_____

_____

2.  Examine your current self-image and beliefs about your potential. Are there any limiting mindsets holding you back from embracing your true worth and capabilities?

_____

_____

_____

_____

_____

_____

3.  When was the last time you engaged in a deep, honest introspection of your thoughts, emotions, and values? What insights did you uncover, and how can

you use that self-awareness to drive meaningful change?

_____

_____

_____

_____

_____

_____

4.   Where do you see a need for greater discipline and structure? What specific goals or habits can you focus on to build a stronger foundation for success?

_____

_____

_____

_____

_____

_____

5.   Reflect on a time when you took full ownership of a situation, whether it was a success or a failure. How did that experience shape your mindset and approach moving forward? What lessons can you apply to other areas of your life?

_____

_____

_____

"Discipline acts as a means to setting and accomplishing a goal, bringing light to the importance of dedication and perseverance."

# CHAPTER SIX: THE POWER OF ENVIRONMENT

"We do not see things as they are; we see them as we are."
**- Anaïs Nin**

The invisible force that guides our actions, more often than not, is the environment we are in. While qualities like talent, effort, and motivation play pivotal roles, the truth is that over time, our characteristics tend to get overpowered by the world around us. Our habits, our decisions, and our very selves are all heavily influenced by our surroundings. Looking back, I can see how the environment I was in during my younger years directly influenced the direction of my life. The idea of fast money and the promise of respect and status within the streets drew me in because that's what success looked like in my environment. The explosive temper and the willingness to resort to violence weren't just personality quirks. They were survival mechanisms in my ruthless reality.

It wasn't until I stepped into a new environment filled with entrepreneurs, visionary leaders, and a culture of abundance that I began to see things clearly. Suddenly, the possibilities that had once seemed distant or unattainable became possible. Our environment doesn't just shape our actions - it shapes our identity. It's the force that either expands or hinders our perception of what's possible. When I found myself, surrounded by the street life I was trying to leave behind, I couldn't help but feel like a caged eagle longing to soar. The discouragement, the depression, the persistent pull back towards the hustle; all stemmed from the fact that my environment didn't align with the vision I held for my life.

But the moment I stepped into that life-changing seminar at the Bronner Bros Hair Show (*The Secrets of a 6-Figure Barber*), everything shifted. Suddenly, I was surrounded by men who looked like me, who shared my background, and who were unapologetically living the type of life I had only dared to dream of. They weren't just making a comfortable living as barbers - they were building six-figure empires, driving luxury cars, and dressing in tailored suits. At that moment, the sense of possibility that had eluded me for so long came rushing back, and I knew that if they could do it, so could I.

*The Power of Expansion*

It's a powerful realization, isn't it? The environment in which we find ourselves can either help us reach our potential faster or hold us back. When we find ourselves in an environment that aligns with our highest dreams and nurtures our growth and development, it's as if the world opens up before us, revealing new avenues of opportunity and fulfillment. But when we're stuck in an environment that constantly reinforces our limitations and drags us back towards old patterns and self-sabotaging behaviors, it can feel like a hamster running on a mini treadmill going nowhere fast, never quite able to break free. This is why the *circle of influence* concept is so important. It's about taking a deep look at the people, places, and things that occupy our attention and asking ourselves: are these factors elevating me towards my goals, or are they keeping me tied to my past? Because make no mistake: what we expose ourselves to has an impact on our thoughts, our emotions, our aspirations, and ultimately, our actions.

The legendary motivational speaker Jim Rohn once said, "You are the same person today as you will be tomorrow. The only difference is the books you read and the people that you continuously associate with." Let that sink in for a moment! The books we read, the social media feeds we scroll through, and the conversations we engage in are programming our minds, shaping our beliefs, and dictating the direction of our lives. We have to understand that what entertains us also trains us. If we aren't careful about surrounding ourselves with positive influences, we might fall back into old habits and ways of thinking we're trying to leave behind. I know this all too well. When I was about to leave the streets behind and start a new career as a barber, I found myself struggling. The barbershop felt stagnant, the money was tight, and I couldn't help but feel the allure of the hustle calling me back. In that moment of doubt and discouragement, I had to choose: would I give in to the familiar, or would I rise to the occasion and do the difficult work of improving my environment?

### The Ripple Effect of Environment

The influence of the environment goes way beyond our growth and development. It's a force that can shape entire communities and affect generations to come. Think about it: in my community, the streets had become a ground for violence, addiction, and hopelessness. The lack of positive examples, the lack of resources, and the belief that destructive behaviors like drug usage and violence are normal were all evidence of an environment that does not support success. Seeing the effect of this on my peers and my family members, I was forced to make adjustments. I knew that if I truly wanted to break the cycle, I had to be willing to do the hard work of creating something different.

Also, in addition to my change, I became deeply committed to developing environments that could serve others. I put my heart and soul into building a barber school, barbershops, and multiple businesses. They weren't just a place of business but a place of mentorship and growth. I invited young men on the edge of the streets to come in, to experience the power of a supportive environment, and to see for themselves that there was another way to get money. And the results were very encouraging. I saw men who had once been consumed by anger, despair, and a sense of hopelessness begin to blossom, rediscovering their self-worth and their dreams. They started saving money, investing in their education, and even starting their own businesses. As these individual changes compounded, I could see how one positive change could lead to many more. This proves the simple truth that John C. Maxwell captured in his book, *The 15 Invaluable Laws of Growth*: "Growth thrives in conducive environments." Just as mold can only thrive in an environment conducive to its growth, and an apple tree can only reach its full potential in the right soil and climate, our personal growth and evolution are linked to the world we live in. The same laws apply to us.

*The Importance of Intentionality*

We often find ourselves allowing our environment to shape us without examining the forces at play. We mindlessly scroll through social media, consuming content that may be subtly (or not-so-subtly eroding our self-esteem and worldview. We spend time with friends and family who may be negative or hold us back. And we wonder why we can't seem to break free from the weight of our problems. But when we intentionally shape our environment with purpose, the results can be extraordinary. It's about taking a step back, assessing the various elements that make up our habitat, and then making conscious choices to create a power that aligns with our highest aspirations. We must be more selective about the people we allow into our inner circle, prioritizing relationships with those who challenge us to grow. We need people who inspire us to dream bigger and then hold us accountable to our commitments. We must be willing to audit our relationships.

This means that you must weigh and evaluate whether your relationships push you forward or hold you back. Are they lifting you or holding you down? Once you've analyzed relationships, it's time to improve them. You will have to totally remove some relationships, while you have to feed and nurture the good ones. One of my mottos is, "If I can't build with you, I can't chill with you." No more meaningless distractions. Also, we may have to be mindful of the media we consume, consciously choosing uplifting, empowering content that nourishes our minds and spirits. I stopped listening to the radio while driving and played nothing but audiobooks and listened to podcasts. That hack alone swiftly changed my life. Did you know that the average person spends 293 hours driving each year, according to a new survey conducted by the AAA Foundation for Traffic Safety? That's almost 2 weeks spent in your car every year! Imagine how much you could learn about a desired topic if you simply changed your approach to something as simple as your daily commute! A change like this is only a minor example of the habits we can change to move closer toward our goals. For us to grow, we must make bold, uncomfortable decisions, like walking away from a familiar but toxic environment in pursuit of greener pastures.

The truth is we all have the power to shape the environments that shape us. This realization isn't just for us – it can inspire others and create positive changes in our communities. So, my challenge for you is to take an honest look at your environment. What aspects of it help you grow, and which ones hold you back? Where can you upgrade, expand, and create an ecosystem supporting your dreams and expanding your gifts? When we take charge of our environment, we open up endless possibilities for ourselves and for making a difference in the world.

## Chapter Summary

This chapter emphasizes our environment's impact on shaping human behavior and personal outcomes. The author draws from his experiences to illustrate how the streets initially held him back, as those environments reinforced limiting beliefs and self-destructive patterns. However, stepping into new environments filled with successful entrepreneurs and visionary mentors produced a shift in his mindset and direction in and of life. He also explains the concept of the *circle of influence*. How the people, places, and things we surround ourselves with directly program our thoughts, emotions, and actions.

**Reflection Questions:**

1.  Examine the various environments you currently occupy - your home, workplace, social circles, online spaces, etc. Which ones are serving your personal growth, and which ones may be holding you back?

_____

_____

_____

_____

_____

2.  Who are the key individuals in your _circle of influence?_ How can you be more intentional about cultivating relationships with people who challenge you to grow and expand your vision?

_____

_____

_____

_____

_____

_____

3.  What bold decisions or changes might you need to make to upgrade your environment and

surround yourself with more nourishing, empowering conditions?

_____

_____

_____

_____

_____

4.   Reflecting on the author's experience of transforming his barbershop into a community hub, how can you apply a similar approach to creating environments that uplift and empower others in your life?

_____

_____

_____

_____

_____

5.   What specific steps can you take today to begin to curate an environment that is truly conducive to the realization of your biggest dreams and aspirations?

_____

_____

_____

"Our environment doesn't just shape our actions - it shapes our identity. It's the force that either expands or hinders our perception of what's possible."

# CHAPTER SEVEN: FROM TRAUMA TO TRIUMPH

"The greatest glory in living lies not in never falling, but in rising every time we fall." - **Nelson Mandela**

When you stop to think about it, the people we often consider to be the greatest among us - the trailblazers, the visionaries, the game-changers - are those who have weathered the most dangerous storms. They emerged from adversity stronger and more resilient than ever. It's the individuals who have stared down their demons, confronted their deepest fears and insecurities, and refused to be defined by the traumas they've endured who ultimately leave a permanent mark on the world. I remember back in 2016, I was leasing a shop from a woman, and we were supposed to split the power bill in half because she owned the building and stayed in the apartment above the shop. Good deal, right?

Wrong. She didn't keep her word, so I ended up getting stuck with the entire bill for 2 years straight, and she refused to make any timely repairs. On top of that, she refused to fix the whole bathroom floor causing it to cave and many other things. So, I ended up being forced to close the shop. A big two-month gap prevented me from operating a professional business. I was depressed, frustrated, losing clients, and on top of that, I got a call that my little brother got shot and killed a few days later. I almost gave up and gave in to the pressure. But one day, a buddy who was familiar with my circumstances at the time was driving downtown and noticed a building for sale. He picked me up, and we went to check out the building. We called the number on the building, and an agent came by to show us the property.

Coincidentally, the gentleman who owned the building was my first criminal lawyer at 17 years old. He ended up renting me the building downtown and four years later I moved down the street and bought a building for my barber shop. Less than a week after the grand opening of the new barber shop, my best friend and I were gunned down. He didn't make it out alive. Now, I own a 12,500 sq ft commercial building where I set up my barber school, salon suites, clothing store, and office space that I rent out to an attorney. Talk about things coming full circle.

It is amazing to see how God works. In most cases, perceived stumbling blocks end up turning into steppingstones on the path to greatness. I thought it was over, but I was just getting started. Trauma may appear to be nothing more than a series of bad experiences that leave us shattered and overwhelmed. The loss of a loved one, the aftermath of abuse, the crippling weight of financial hardship - these are crushing blows that can feel like they're ripping the very foundation out from under us. And in those raw, vulnerable moments, it's understandable to want to curl up and hide, to give in to the temptation to let our pain define us.

But what if I told you that those traumas, those moments of suffering, are often the very things that propel us toward our greatest triumphs? Overcoming challenges can be crucial to finding our true strength and purpose. In adversity, we're forced to confront our deepest fears and insecurities. It's when we're pushed to the edge that we're forced to dig deeper, to tap into reserves of strength and determination we never knew we possessed. And it's through the difficult process of picking up the pieces and rebuilding our lives that we discover the true measure of our character, the full scope of our potential. I know this because it's a journey I've walked myself. The traumas I've endured that permeated my environment and nearly broke me: the shootings, the loss of loved ones, the constant threat of violence.

There were times when I felt so shattered, so consumed by the weight of my circumstances, that the idea of a brighter future seemed like nothing more than false hope.

Something deep within me refused to give up. Perhaps it was the unshakable faith that had anchored me during the darkest times, or the stubborn determination forged by years of battling against the odds. Whatever it was, it pushed me to keep moving forward, face my fears and insecurities head-on, and transform the tragedies that nearly broke me into the strength that led me to my biggest victories. And let me tell you, it wasn't an easy journey by any stretch of the imagination. There were countless moments of doubt, anguish, and feeling utterly lost and alone. I had to admit the hard truth that I was my biggest problem, so I became the solution. It was this humbling process that ultimately led to my transformation.

Through that journey of self-examination and accountability, I began to uncover the source of my real strength, my real power that was dormant all along. I realized that the very challenges I had once seen as unsettling were, in fact, the building blocks of my empowerment. Each scar, and moment of pain, had prepared me to become a stronger version of myself - someone who was unafraid to dream big, to push limits, and to refuse to be defined by the tragedies of the past. The fog of despair and self-limitation began to lift, and I found a renewed sense of purpose and determination. I no longer saw myself as a product of my environment, a victim of circumstance, but rather as the architect of my destiny

- someone with the power to transform not just my own life but the lives of those around me.

Think about the lives of the true trailblazers, the visionaries who have left a permanent mark on the world. So many of them have weathered incredible storms, faced unimaginable odds, and emerged from those crucibles of adversity stronger and wiser than ever before. They're the ones who have refused to be defined by their traumas, who have instead chosen to harness that pain and transform it into fuel for their evolution and the betterment of humanity. Take Nelson Mandela, for example, who spent 27 years behind bars, enduring unbearable hardship and oppression, and yet, upon his release, emerged as one of the most influential and inspiring leaders. Or consider the countless civil rights pioneers, like Malcolm X and others, who faced violence, imprisonment, and even death in their pursuit of justice and equality. These individuals didn't allow their traumas to break them - instead, they channeled that pain into a relentless drive to create a better world. Take Oprah Winfrey, who endured a childhood of abuse and neglect only to rise to become one of the most influential media moguls of our time.

The common thread that binds these stories of triumph is the belief that our traumas, no matter how long, can be transformed into the very fuel that propels us toward our greatest successes. As I reflect on my journey, from the depths of the streets to the heights of entrepreneurship and community leadership, I can't help but marvel at the role that trauma has played in shaping my path. Without the trials and tribulations I've endured, without the scars that have become the very bricks that built my life's story, I wouldn't be the person I am today. The resilience, determination, and sense of purpose now guide every step I take.

This realization has shaped the way I approach my own life and the lives of those I aim to uplift and inspire. I believe, with every fiber of my being, that the capacity to overcome adversity is not just a skill but a superpower that can be harnessed to achieve greatness, create positive change, and break the limitations we so often place on ourselves. And so, my challenge to you is to embrace your traumas not as burdens to obstruct your path but as opportunities to lift you. To confront your fears and insecurities with the bold, unwavering belief that on the other side of your greatest challenges awaits a version of yourself that is stronger and wiser than you ever imagined possible.

## Chapter Summary

This chapter explores the powerful potential within our traumas and adversities, positioning them as the gateway that lends us entry into our greatest triumphs. He draws from his personal experiences, sharing how the challenges he faced, from shootings to the loss of loved ones, could have easily broken him but instead became the push for his turnaround.

## Reflection Questions:

1.  What are some of the significant traumas or adversities you've faced in your own life? How have they shaped the person you are today?

_____

_____

_____

_____

_____

2.  In what ways have you witnessed the power of resilience and determination in the face of adversity, either in your own life or the lives of others?

_____

_____

_____

_____

_____

_____

3.  Reflect on the stories of renowned trailblazers and visionaries mentioned in the chapter. What lessons can you draw from their ability to transform their traumas into fuel for their greatest achievements?

_____

_____

_____

_____

_____

4.   What fears or insecurities have you been
hesitant to confront? How might embracing a spirit
of vulnerability and accountability unlock new
avenues of personal growth and empowerment?

_____

_____

_____

_____

_____

5.   What steps can you take to consciously
channel the pain of your past traumas into positive,
purposeful action toward your greatest aspirations?

_____

_____

_____

_____

_____

"Confront your fears and insecurities with the bold, unwavering belief that on the other side of your greatest challenges awaits a version of yourself that is stronger and wiser than you ever imagined possible."

# CHAPTER EIGHT: ONWARD AND UPWARD

"The future belongs to those who believe in the beauty of their dreams." - **Eleanor Roosevelt**

As we come to the end of this journey, I feel incredibly grateful. What began as a personal narrative of struggles has become something more. The overcoming of obstacles with intention has become a guidebook for discovering the boundless potential dormant within each of us. Through the sharing of my experiences, we have peeled back the layers of trauma, self-doubt, and limiting beliefs that have kept so many trapped in cycles of self-doubt, disbelief, and self-distraction. But more importantly, we have uncovered the core principles and strategies that can take us from Trauma to Triumph.

*The Power of Purpose*

At the heart of this lies the rediscovery of our deepest purpose. When lose touch with our Why - the driving force that compels us to leap out of bed each morning - we become susceptible to the allure of worldly validation, material gain, and short-term pleasures. We lose sight of the unique gifts and talents meant to be shared with the world, becoming mere passengers in our own lives.

However, as we have explored throughout this book, true and lasting fulfillment is only found by aligning our actions with our highest callings. It is in the pursuit of our purpose that we tap into a wellspring of passion, creativity, and unwavering determination. Purpose becomes the beacon of light guiding us through life's storms, the North Star illuminating our path even in the presence of uncertainty.

*A Personal Revelation*

During my toughest moments, my purpose became clear when I found myself staring down the barrel of a gun, both as the victim and the potential perpetrator. It was a gut-wrenching experience that made me realize my choices didn't just affect me, but also those I cared about the most. This shattered the false beliefs I held and ultimately sparked a beautiful change. I realized then that my true purpose transcended the petty trappings of the streets - the flashy possessions, the all-too fleeting respect, and the promise of easy money.

Instead, my calling was to be a beacon of hope, a living testament to the power of redemption. My mission became clear: to use my own journey to inspire and empower others who, like me, were caught in destructive cycles and needed a way out.

## *Embracing Purpose*

When I began to align my thoughts, habits, and actions with this newfound purpose, the floodgates of possibility opened wide. Doors once firmly shut were now swung wide, offering me opportunities to pursue my dreams and make a tangible impact on my community. It felt as if the universe was conspiring to support my change, rewarding my courage and commitment with a series of breakthroughs.

In conclusion, this chapter isn't just about my personal victories, but about sharing hope with everyone going through tough times. When we live with a clear purpose, we can transform challenges into triumphs. As we move on to the next part of our journey, remember these lessons and know that we all have the power to overcome difficulties and achieve our dreams. My life is proof of that.

## Chapter Summary

In this chapter, we follow the author's journey from struggle to discovery of purpose. Initially recounting personal challenges, the author transforms these experiences into a guidebook for unlocking personal potential. The author reveals layers of self-doubt and obstacles common to many, emphasizing the importance of discovering one's true purpose. The chapter explores how losing touch with one's *why* can lead to seeking superficial rewards like approval or money. Real fulfillment, however, comes from aligning actions with one's deepest passions and talents. The author shares a pivotal moment of realization during a difficult experience. This moment highlighted the impact of their choices on others and sparked a shift in priorities away from material gains toward becoming a beacon of hope and change.

By embracing their purpose, the author experiences significant personal growth and unexpected opportunities. The narrative illustrates how focusing on a clear mission can transform challenges into opportunities for growth and success.

## Reflection Questions:

1. What does the author mean by finding your purpose? How does knowing your purpose help in overcoming challenges?

_____

_____

_____

_____

2. How did the author's toughest moments lead to a clearer understanding of his mission in life?

_____

_____

_____

_____

_____

3. According to this chapter, why is it important to align your actions with your deepest passions and talents?

_____

_____

_____

_____

_____

4. Can you think of a time when you or someone you know faced a difficult situation? How did they find strength or purpose during that time?

_____

_____

_____

_____

_____

_____

_____

5. What do you think the author means by "turning challenges into triumphs?" Can you give an example from your own life or someone else's where this happened?

_____

_____

_____

_____

_____

# ABOUT THE AUTHOR

Lorenzo "Zo" William's life proves the transformative power of the human spirit. Born and raised in the streets of Mt. Vernon, Illinois, his journey has been anything but ordinary. From the moment he became a father, he found himself confronted with a choice: yield to the pull of the streets or rise above the limitations of his circumstances and follow a new path. Regrettably, he initially fell prey to the hustle like so many young men in his position. Desperate to provide for his new family, he went into the underground world of drugs and violence, quickly earning a reputation as a formidable player in the game. But higher stakes mean higher risks. He began to experience a desire - a voice that refused to be silenced, urging him to do better, to be better.

He was shot not once but twice, in two different situations and he came very close to death. He also lost his brother and best friend to the same dangerous circumstances that nearly took his life. Many people would have given up after going through so much pain and difficulty, but Zo was relentless in the pursuit of wanting more for his life.

Surprisingly, even to himself, he found the strength to make a brave decision to change his life. He had to look deep inside himself and completely change how he saw himself and the world around him. Through hard work and a commitment to improving himself, Zo started to break free from the beliefs and habits that had been holding him back.

He realized that true freedom could only come if he took responsibility for his role in creating the chaos in his life. With this new understanding, he worked hard to become a new person who lived according to his values and purpose. He became a student, learning from spiritual teachers, self-help experts, and business mentors. Each lesson and breakthrough helped him move forward on the path of change he wanted.

As Zo's thoughts and perspectives changed, his life changed, too. He went from being a lost young man to a focused, disciplined, and ambitious entrepreneur. Through determination and hard work, he built a successful business empire that includes a barbershop, a barber college, commercial real estate, and other businesses. He also repaired his important relationships, becoming a devoted husband and father to his nine children.

Now he has dedicated himself to uplifting the next generation, using the example of his own life experiences as a beacon of hope and inspiration for

the young people in his community. *Trauma To Triumph: Never Give Up* isn't merely a catchy title; it's his authentic story.